I dedicate this book to
Mom, Tracie, and Sedona

Hello, I'm Sammy the Frog

And this is my sister's pretty pink dog.

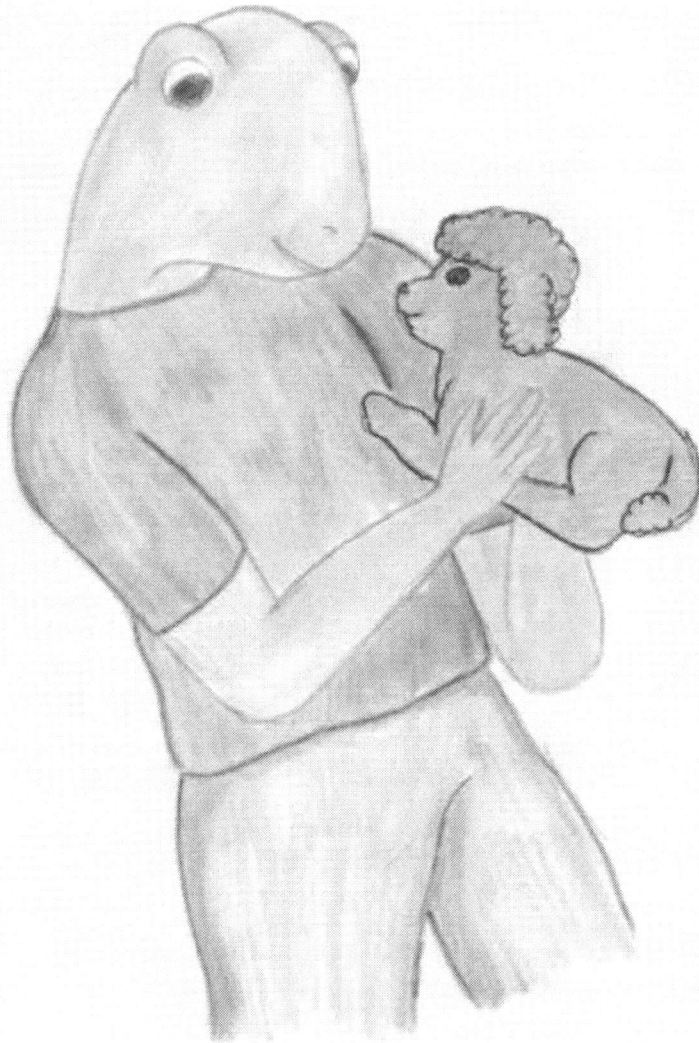

My sister's name is Lily and she loves to be silly.

She also loves to play in the pool.

And learn new things in school.

Today she is learning how to
plant pretty pink flowers.

To give her special princess power's.

To show her friend Sedona
the real power of a special princess.

First, you must always say please and thank you.

Especially when a princess get's
an extra special gift, or a little gift every day.

Because being polite is the only way
to have princess power every day.

Thank You.

One Sunday, Funday; we took Lily's pretty pink dog for a walk on a trail on Grand Island, MI.

Lily and Sedona found a rock filled with glitter.

And they gave it to me for luck
to keep away the BIG critters.

But luckily, we were able to ride a duck.

Which was a lot of fun because we were flying high in the sky.

But when we were done
Lily's pretty pink dog was gone.

We looked left and we looked right.

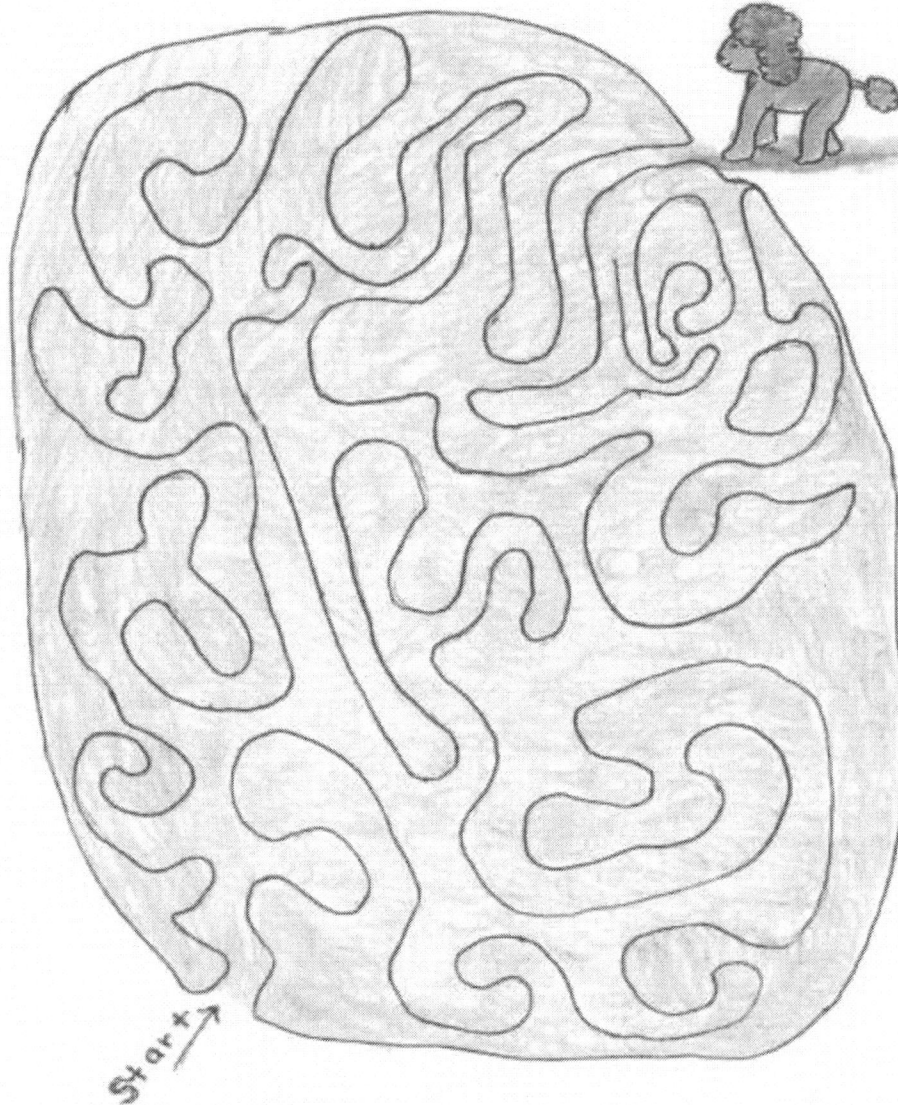

Start →

We looked high and we looked low.

But we had no luck at all. We didn't even have the rock filled with glitter.

Or Lily's pink dog.
Not even luck to keep away the BIG critters.

So we marched and marched all day till we found a treehouse in the middle of the bay.

And Lily's pretty pink dog sitting on hay on top of a huge rock on Lake Superior.

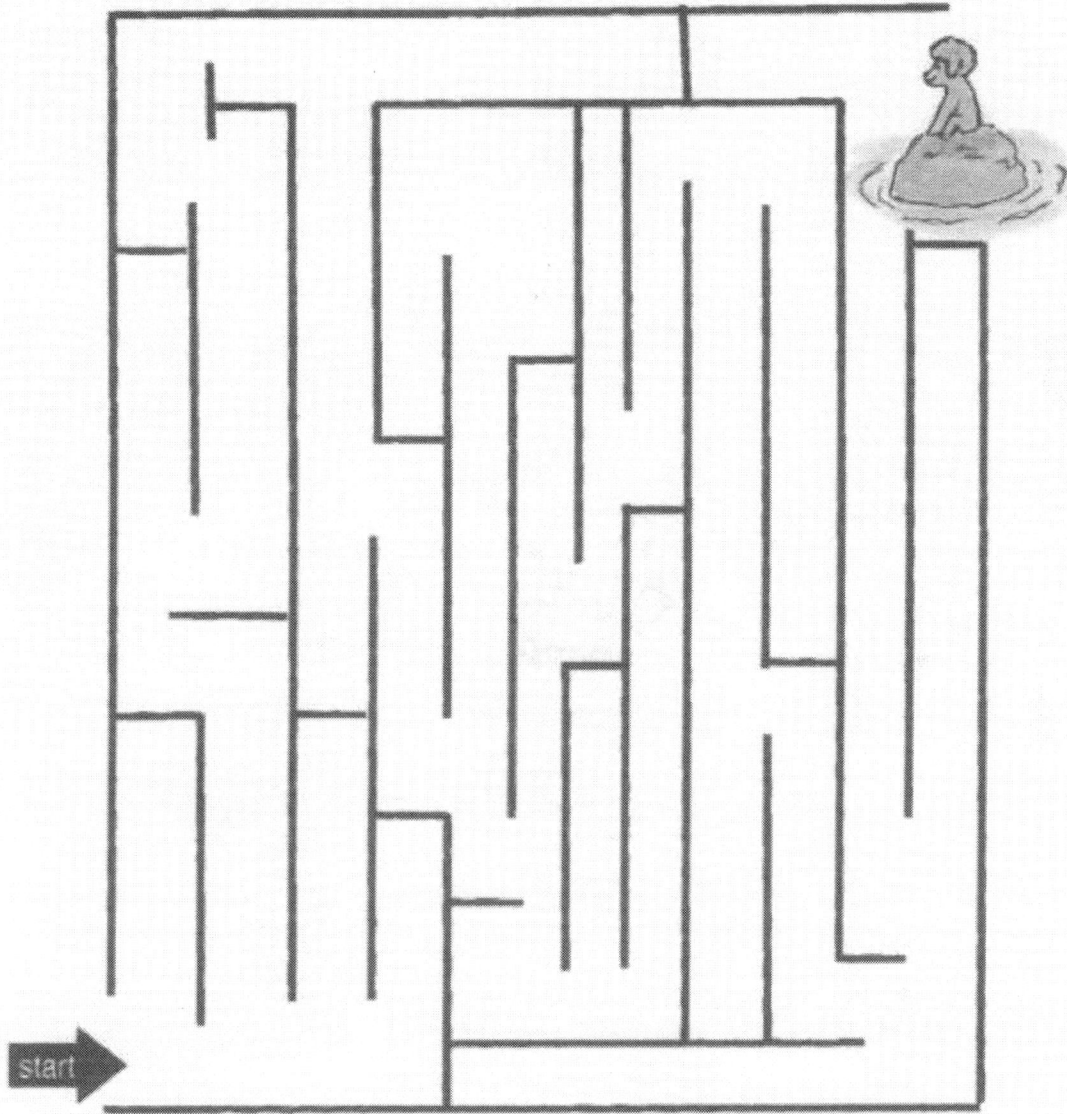

Meditating about a special way to tell us that she has a place to stay.

Here in the treehouse with her family
and how important it is to love and pray.

Because Lily's pretty pink dog can only bark;
she cannot talk like you and me.

She can only have faith and trust in God
to show us all the places we need to be.

And remember the special princess power when you may plant a pretty pink flower.

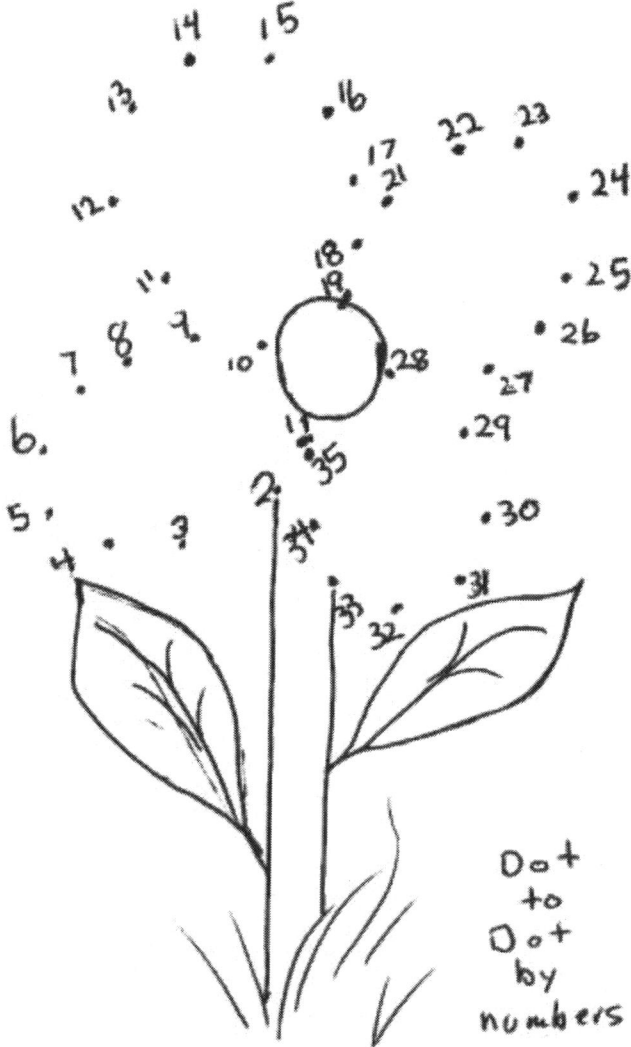

Dot
to
Dot
by
numbers

1 Corinthians 13:8
"Love never ends"

About the Author

Jamie Chester grew up in Muskegon, Michigan. Her inspiration came from her love for her daughter Sedona, the love for their dog Storm, the love for their parakeet Bobbi's, and the many beautiful places they have explored in Michigan.

About the Illustrator

Dawn Evans grew up in White Cloud, Michigan. She loves painting and little animals. Her inspiration came from her precious and beautiful granddaughter.

30936023R00017

Made in the USA
San Bernardino, CA
26 February 2016